Michael Cohen

I REMEMBER

FOR VOICE AND PIANO

Text by

Enid Futterman
Based on the Diary of Anne Frank

LAUREN KEISER
MUSIC PUBLISHING

Michael Cohen was born in New York City and studied composition with Harold Shapero and Irving Fine. A graduate of Brandeis University *cum laude* and the Dalcroze School of Music, his diverse career as a composer encompasses works for chamber ensemble, musical theater, opera and television.

Cohen's three related pieces based on Anne Frank's diary, *I Remember, Yours, Anne,* and *I Am Anne Frank,* have received distinguished performances throughout the United States, Canada, Europe , South America, and Japan. The works have also enjoyed premieres in prestigious venues including Lincoln Center in New York City and the US Holocaust Memorial Museum in Washington, DC. His discography includes two celebrated CD releases for the chamber version of *I Remember,* first by Newport Classics, followed by a 2009 independent release by Canadian flute artist Brenda Fedoruk, who also features Cohen's *From the Wall* in a world premiere recording on the same album.

Michael Cohen's other credits include his nomination as finalist in a New York City Opera Competition for *Rappaccini's Daughter,* a nationally-televised appearance of his scoring and arrangement, *A Passover Seder,* presented by Elie Weisel, and numerous commissions from the Concert Artists Guild, Serenata, Music Amici, the Manhattan Brass Quintet, and the trio Windsong. His *Two Songs on Texts by Edna St.Vincent Millay* was premiered at the Bowdoin Summer Music Festival in Maine.

♬

Enid Futterman's work has received the Richard Rodgers Production Award, the Seagram's New Music Theater Award, and grants from the Ford Foundation and National Endowment for the Arts. She has written the text for three musical pieces based on the diaries of Anne Frank, all in collaboration with composer Michael Cohen. She is the lyricist and book writer of the musical versions of *Portrait of Jennie* (with Howard Marren) and *An Open Window* (with Sarah Ackerman).

Futterman's work has been performed off-Broadway, as well as in theaters around the US, and in the UK, the Netherlands, South Africa, Belgium, and Japan. Ms. Futterman is also the author and photographer of *Bittersweet Journey,* a novel. She lives in Claverack, New York, where she publishes and edits *Our Town,* a quarterly magazine, with her partner, John Isaacs.

Foreword

I Remember was commissioned in 1995 for the US Holocaust Memorial Museum's Chamber Music Series, but its origins date back a couple of decades earlier, to the inception of a musical theater piece based on the diaries of Anne Frank, called *Yours, Anne.* I Remember is based on that score, and uses much of the same musical and lyrical material, but as a chamber piece, originally written for voice, flute, harp and cello, it is very much its own work. This new version, for voice and piano, makes the work available to singers who have no access to a chamber ensemble, while retaining the essential lyricism of the piece.

Since its premiere performance in Washington in early 1996, *I Remember* has been recorded twice, and performed over fifty times, at Weill Recital Hall, Ravinia, Noordekerk in Amsterdam, and many other venues in the US, UK, Canada, and the Netherlands. In twenty-four minutes, *I Remember* makes no attempt to tell all of Anne's stories, but instead distills her diaries to tell the stories of the inner life of a remarkable young writer.

Enid Futterman, 2009

I REMEMBER

for Voice and Piano

Text by **ENID FUTTERMAN**
(based on the diaries of Anne Frank)

Music by **MICHAEL COHEN**

Andante
mp quasi recitativo
Voce
Piano
mf
Dear Kit - ty, I am thir-teen years
old. It seems to me that no one will be in - t'rested in what I write,
and yet I have to write; some-thing is bur - ied deep in-side my soul.
mp
poco accel.
poco rit.
a tempo
quasi recitativo

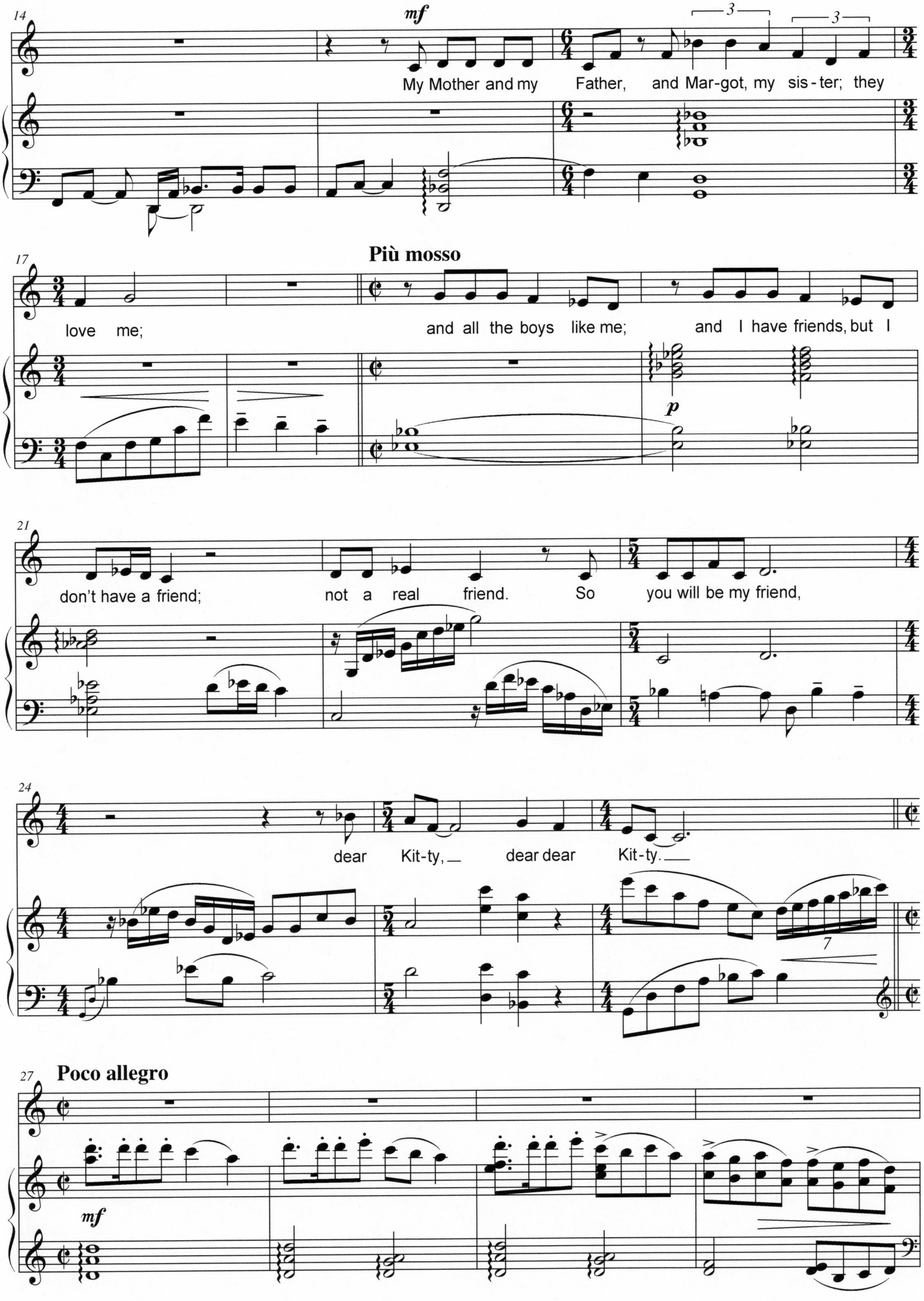
mf
My Mother and my Father, and Mar-got, my sis-ter; they love me;
Più mosso
and all the boys like me; and I have friends, but I don't have a friend; not a real friend.
p
So you will be my friend, dear Kit-ty, dear dear Kit-ty.
Poco allegro
mf

31
mf
I will tell you stor - ies; I will tell you ev' - ry - thing; I will show you all my feel - ings.
mp
34
You will be my con - science; you will be my con - fi - dante;
mp
37
rit.
a tempo
you will keep my deep - est sec - rets.
mf
41
My thoughts, my dreams, my plans.
f legato

44
49
Dear Kit - ty,
p
espress.
54
espress.
mf
57
molto allarg.
pp sub.
Deliberato
61
ff
sfz
66
mp legato

69
mf
I sup-
71
-pose you would like to hear, what it feels like to dis-ap-pear; I don't
73
know yet.
I don't think I will e-ver feel at
p
7
75
home here.
mp
It's like a ho - li-day
pp
78
in the most pe-cul - iar board-ing house,
legato
3
3

poco rit.
mp
but it's
a tempo
mp
more of an adven-ture; ro - man - tic, int'resting, dar - ing,
p
mp
f
f
dan - ger-ous.
ppp sub.
ff
sfz
mf
pesante
molto rit.
a tempo
pp
mp
8
loco

104
mp
It's like a little light, sus - pended in the darkness, sur -
p
108
-rounded by the dark - ness.
mp
112
pp
119
mp
Sometimes, I laugh; somehow, I hide; I nev - er, e - ver, go out -
pp
ppp
126
Allegro con moto
- side.
pp
mf

131
mf
Dear Kit - ty, I am long-ing, long-ing to
136
have a friend, to be a - lone, to talk, to cry. I be -
mf
140
-lieve that the sun is shin - ing; I feel sun - light shin-ing; I am
mf
7
f
144
rest - less, breath-less, don't know what to say, don't know what to read, what to write,
Ped.
*

148
what to do. I on-ly know that I am long-ing, ach-ing to
152
see the world, to be myself, to breathe, to fly.
molto rit.
a tempo
156
I be-lieve it is spring with-in me;
159
I feel spring with-in me; I am diz-zy, craz-y,

molto rit.
don't know what to do, don't know how to be, what to think, how to feel. I
Andante
on - ly know long-ing, long-ing,
pp
rit.
a tempo
pp
long - ing.
ppp
Ped.
cresc.
poco accel.
Con moto

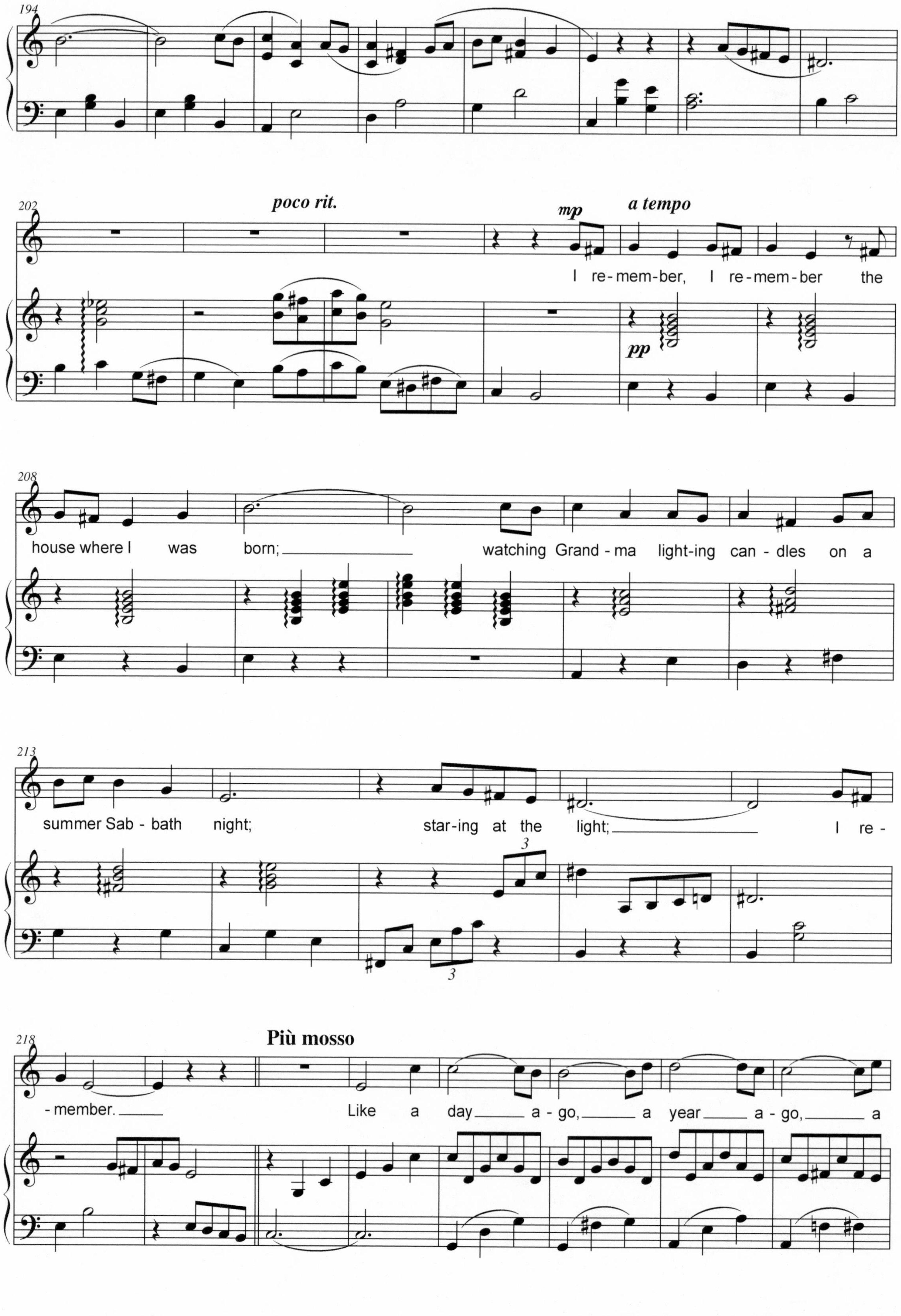
194
202
poco rit.
mp
a tempo
I re-mem-ber, I re-mem-ber the
pp
208
house where I was born;
watching Grand-ma light-ing can-dles on a
213
summer Sab-bath night;
star-ing at the light;
I re-
218
Più mosso
-member.
Like a day a-go, a year a-go, a

226
life a - go, so clear-ly, so vague-ly, so dear-ly, so
234
poco rit.
a tempo
rit.
long-ing - ly; I re-mem - ber, and I for - get.
242
a tempo
I re - mem - ber, I re - mem - ber the house where I was
p
247
molto allarg.
born; I re - mem - ber, I re - mem - ber the world where I was born;
f
252
Meno mosso
there was mus - ic, there was sun - light, there was life on ev - 'ry street;
3
3
3

poco rit.
a tempo
ev- 'ry dream was sweet;
I re - mem - ber,
I re - mem-ber,
I re-mem - ber.
quasi cadenza
sfz
f
molto rit.
pesante
sfz
Andante
pp
mf
Dark... night, cold... eyes;
dark eyes;
big dark eyes in the
cluster
pp
f sub.
p

295
mf
Ossia: octave lower
night. No face, no light, on-ly eyes; huge and hungry eyes; she
pp
p
300
nev-er said a word but I heard what she said with her eyes:
Spoken: Oh, Anne, you have deserted me.
Why have you deserted me?
ff
poco a poco cresc. et accel.
304
mp
Why me? Help me; oh, God, I have de-sert-ed her; why have I de-sert-ed her?
p
307
Why her? Help her; save her from her hell.

Deliberato
No face, no hair, on-ly eyes; on-ly eyes and bones.
Spoken (ad lib.):
It was me.
She was me.
Oh, God.
Tempo I (Andante)
Dear Kit - ty,
I am fifteen years old.
I don't want to be like Mar - got, and Moth - er, and Miss - es van Daan,
and all of the women who work all their lives, and are for -
legato

Poco agitato
-gotten.
I'm afraid of the dark;
I'm alone in the dark;
poco a poco cresc. et accel.
I see something buried deep in - side my soul.
espress.
Andante
gliss.
Più mosso
pp sub.
rit.
a tempo

359
364
Andante
I'm facing my- self; I'm facing the
370
night; I know what I want, I know who I am, as long as I
373
Più mosso
write. I can re - cap-ture ev' - rything as long as I know I can write; I
376
poco rit.
a tempo
know I can write; I know who I am; I see myself whole; as

good as my heart, as bad as my dreams, as old as my soul. I can i-
- mag - ine an - y-thing as long as I know I'm a-live;
molto rit.
Andante maestoso
I still love life.
This page is blank.
rit.
Adagio
I am Anne Frank.
Allegro non troppo

405
411
cresc.
417
f
ff
422
rit.
Andante
pp
426
mp espress.
429
mf
Dear Kit - ty, I see the

432
world turning in - to a wil - der-ness.
435
Dear Kit - ty,
I hear the ev - er approach-ing
pp
Ped.
438
thun - der;
I feel the
Con moto
cresc. poco a poco
suf - fer - ing of peop-le be - ing torn a-part, and
441
yet, in spite of ev - 'ry-thing, I still be - lieve that peop-le are
445
good at heart; I still be - lieve that someday this war will end;
f
espress.

450
3
pp sub.
we will see peace a - gain, go home a - gain; I
pp sub.
455
still be - lieve what I can.
Yours,
Andante
463
Anne.
pp
469
475
mp
pp